SNAIL

John Woodward

CHELSEA CLUBHOUSE

An Imprint of Chelsea House Publishers

Snail

Chelsea Clubhouse
An imprint of Chelsea House
132 West 31st Street
New York, NY 10001

Library of Congress Cataloging-in-Publication Data
Woodward, John.
  Snail / John Woodward.
      p. cm. -- (Garden minibeasts up close)
  Includes index.
  ISBN 978-1-60413-900-6
  1. Snails--Juvenile literature. I. Title. II. Series.
  QL430.4.W668 2010
  594'.3--dc22
                              2009054104

Chelsea Clubhouse books are available at special discounts when purchased in bulk quantities for businesses, associations, institutions, or sales promotions. Please call our Special Sales Department in New York at (212) 967-8800 or (800) 322-8755.

You can find Chelsea Clubhouse on the World Wide Web at http://www.chelseahouse.com

Produced for Chelsea House by Discovery Books
Managing Editor: Laura Durman
Project Editor: Clare Collinson
Designer: Blink Media
Illustrator: Jim Chanell

Photo acknowledgments: Corbis: pp 15, 19 (Visuals Unlimited), 21 (Arthur Morris); FLPA: pp 11 (Norbert Wu/Minden Pictures), 16 (Maurice Nimmo), 25 (Chris Mattison), 28 (Nigel Cattlin), 29 (Martin B. Withers); iStockphoto.com: pp 4 (fotek), 7 (Yaroslav Osadchyy), 8 (Achim Prill), 13 (Svetlana Tikhonova), 17 (Willie B. Thomas), 24 (gunschi), 26 (Linda Alstead), 27 (Jozsef Szasz-Fabian); Photoshot: pp 20 (NHPA), 23 (Bruce Coleman); Shutterstock Images: title page (kotomiti), pp 5 (Alexey Biryukov), 9 (IRC), 10 (Sasha Radosavljevich), 11 (Cigdem Cooper), 12 (almondd), 14 (Mircea Bezergheanu), 18 (Mytho), 22 (David Woolfenden).

Cover printed by Bang Printing, Brainerd, MN
Book printed and bound by Bang Printing, Brainerd, MN
Date printed April 2010
Printed in the United States of America

10 9 8 7 6 5 4 3 2 1

Contents

Finding snails

You probably know a snail when you see one. Snails are a type of **mollusk**, with soft, wet bodies and hard, **spiral** shells.

Snails do not like cold or dry weather. They usually come out to feed when it is warm and damp. The best time to look for them is in the evening or in the early morning when there is **dew** on the ground.

Snails feed on plants, so they are easy to find in backyards. Look for them on bushes and trees, among fallen leaves, and in the vegetable garden.

4

When a snail is resting, it pulls its body inside its shell so that it does not dry out.

Did You Know?

There are thousands of different types of snails. Some live on land, but most live in the sea. Others are found in rivers, lakes, and ponds.

During the day, snails usually find a damp place to rest. You can often find them on walls in shady corners or hiding among leaves or stones.

A snail's body

Did you know that snails only have one foot? Their foot is the soft, rubbery part of the body that you can see. At the bottom of the foot is a flat, slimy **sole**.

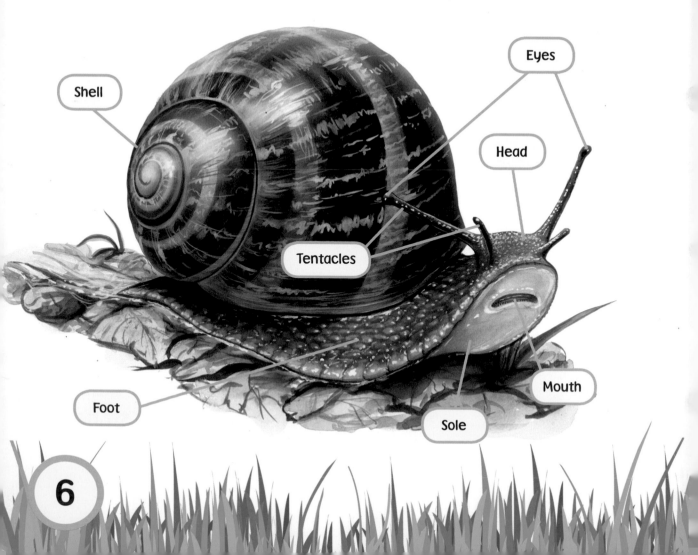

Shell

Eyes

Head

Tentacles

Foot

Sole

Mouth

Most of a snail's **organs** are hidden under its shell. The shell also protects the snail from its enemies.

At the front of a snail's foot is its head. A snail that lives on land has two pairs of **tentacles**, or feelers. At the end of the longer pair are the snail's eyes. Its mouth is on the underside of its head.

The rest of a snail's body is coiled up inside its shell.

Did You Know?

A snail can use a powerful **muscle** in its body to pull the whole foot inside its shell.

Snails and slugs

If you think that slugs are snails that have lost their shells, you are almost right! Slugs and snails are closely related. They have very similar bodies, but slugs do not have big shells on their backs.

Did You Know?
Some slugs do have tiny shells on their backs. But they are so small that they do not help to protect the slug's body.

The front part of a slug's body is covered by a thick layer of skin called the **mantle**. A snail's mantle is usually hidden under its shell.

Mantle

8

Breathing hole

Like all slugs and snails that live on land, the banana slug breathes through a hole in the side of its body. The hole opens and closes as the slug breathes.

Did You Know?

Snails and slugs are the only mollusks that can live on land. All other mollusks—including mussels, scallops, squid, and octopuses—live in water.

Slugs do not have shells to help them keep their bodies moist. So they spend all their time in damp places.

Water snails

Look in any pond, and it is likely you will see snails living in the water. They feed on **algae**. They also eat all sorts of dead material that falls to the bottom of the pond.

Some water snails, like this ramshorn snail, come to the surface to breathe air. Other water snails breathe underwater using **gills**, like those of a fish.

Purple-ring top snails live in the ocean off the west coast of North America. They feed on algae, dead fish, and other sea creatures.

Most of the world's snails and slugs live in the sea. Many sea snails attack and eat other animals. Some, such as tropical cone snails, are armed with a deadly **venom**.

Did You Know?

You may not think of slugs as pretty, but some sea slugs are beautiful. Many are brightly colored to warn their enemies that they are poisonous.

Snail shells

Have you ever found an empty snail shell on the ground? A snail's shell is a spiral tube made of a chalky material called calcium. It has a thin covering, a bit like a coat of **varnish**.

Did You Know?

Snail shells are amazingly tough. They often survive as **fossils** for millions of years. You can find fossils of snail shells that are older than dinosaur fossils!

Snail shells come in many colors, shapes, and sizes. Most are slightly pointed, but some are flat. Others, like the shell of this tree snail, are sharp-pointed **spires**.

The lines on a snail's shell show where each new layer was added to the shell.

As a snail grows older, new layers are added to its shell, so the shell gets bigger and bigger.

When a snail is fully grown, a thick lip forms at the opening of the shell and the shell stops growing.

Sensitive snails

Eye

If you look closely at a land snail, you will see its two pairs of tentacles. These help the snail see, feel, smell, and taste.

A snail sees with the eyes at the end of the longer pair of tentacles.

A snail probably cannot see shapes clearly, but its eyes are good at detecting light and dark. This helps the snail notice passing shadows that might mean it is in danger.

14

Did You Know?

Tentacles are very important to a snail. They help it decide where to go and what to eat. If it senses danger, it can protect its tentacles by quickly pulling them inside its body. It does this by turning them inside out!

Snails use their shorter tentacles to feel their way and pick up smells and tastes.

Water snails have just one pair of tentacles. Their eyes are at the base of the tentacles.

This apple snail lives in water. Its tentacles are very good at detecting smells.

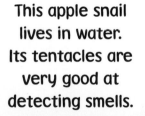

Eye

15

On the move

Snails move very slowly.
As they crawl along, they glide on
a smooth layer of slimy **mucus**.
This helps them move over rough
ground and protects the soft
underside of their bodies.

Did You Know?
A garden snail is the
world's fastest snail.
It can travel as fast as
55 yards an hour! At that
rate, it would take it
32 hours to travel
a mile.

You can tell where a snail has
been by the trail of silvery
slime it leaves behind.

If you see a snail moving, watch carefully. The muscles in its foot lift each part of its body, creating a rippling movement. This pushes the snail forward on the flat sole of its foot.

Hungry snails

Do you like green vegetables? For some snails, they are a favorite food! Most snails feed on dead plants, **fungi**, and algae. Others like to eat juicy leaves, fruit, and flowers. Some snails feed on other animals. They may even attack smaller snails.

Snails can be **pests** in the vegetable garden because they chew holes in the leaves of plants.

If you see a snail eating, listen carefully. You may hear a scraping or scratching sound. Snails have a special tongue called a **radula**. This is covered with thousands of tiny, sharp teeth.

This is a close-up of the teeth on a snail's radula (tongue). A snail uses its teeth to scrape away at food, almost like a cheese grater.

Did You Know?

Slugs can eat twice their own body weight every day. That's like a child eating about 400 quarter-pound burgers!

Enemies and defenses

Snails have lots of enemies. They are eaten by birds, insects, and small animals such as toads and lizards.

When a snail senses danger, it defends itself by pulling its body into its shell.

This hungry lizard is eating a garden snail.

The snail kite of Florida eats almost nothing but water snails. It uses its hooked beak to snip them out of their shells.

Some animals use their strong jaws or beaks to break snail shells open. Then they eat the snail inside.

When a slug wants to protect itself, it oozes a large amount of sticky slime. This can gum up the mouths of its enemies and force them to give up the attack.

Did You Know?

Many people around the world enjoy eating snails, especially when the snails are cooked with butter, garlic, and parsley!

Hiding away

How do snails survive the winter months, when the weather is very cold? Many snails have a long rest, or become **dormant**, during the winter. This is called **hibernation**. They may stay hidden away for many months.

These snails are hibernating in a crack in a tree trunk.

When a snail becomes dormant, it pulls its body into its shell. It seals up the opening with a thick layer of dried mucus.

Snails also become dormant during the summer, if the weather becomes too hot and dry.

The layer of mucus over the opening of a snail's shell helps to keep its body moist while it is dormant.

Breeding

When snails mate, they circle around each other and then curl together and **fertilize** each other's eggs.

Snails usually **mate** once a year, in late spring or early summer.

Most snails have both male and female body parts. After mating, both snails produce eggs.

Snails usually mate on the ground. Giant garden slugs mate while dangling from a tree on a long string of mucus!

Love dart

25

Eggs and young

If you find some tiny white balls hidden in the soil or under a stone, they might be the eggs of a snail. Snails lay up to a hundred eggs a few weeks after mating.

A snail usually lays its eggs when the weather is warm and damp. The eggs begin to hatch about two weeks later.

A few months after hatching, baby snails begin to look like miniature versions of their parents.

When a baby snail hatches from an egg, it has a miniature shell, which often has no color. As it grows, new layers are added and the shell becomes its adult color.

Snails usually become adult within a year, but the biggest types may take four years. Most snails live for between two and eight years.

Did You Know?

The biggest land snails of all are giant African snails. They often grow to about 8 inches in length, but have been known to grow to more than 15 inches!

Snails and people

Many of us think that snails are animals that we could do without. They can be a real problem for gardeners because they eat young plants.

But snails are helpful to people, too. They eat rotting plants, and the waste they produce helps to keep the soil healthy. This makes new plants grow well.

Gardeners often pick snails off their plants by hand. This is one way of stopping snails from eating their plants!

28

Did you know that land snails are sometimes kept as pets? People often keep water snails in **aquariums**, too. The snails help to keep aquariums clean by eating dead matter that falls to the bottom. They also eat algae growing on the glass.

African land snails can do a lot of damage to food crops. It is against the law to keep them as pets in the United States.

Did You Know?

It is illegal to bring snails from other countries into the United States. In 1966, a boy **smuggled** three giant African land snails into Florida. He wanted to keep them as pets, but they got away. After seven years there were 18,000 of them! It cost the state a million dollars to get rid of them.

Glossary

algae: Plant-like, tiny living things that live in water.

aquarium: A tank of water used to keep fish or similar animals.

breed: To multiply by producing young.

courtship: Behavior used by a male or female to attract a mate.

dew: The moisture that appears on grass, and other places, during the night.

dormant: Being in a state of deep sleep that uses very little energy or food.

fertilize: In animals, to add the material that makes an egg develop into a baby.

fossil: The remains of an ancient creature preserved in rock.

fungi: Living things that look a little like plants but feed on the remains of other living things. Mushrooms and toadstools are fungi.

gills: The organs used by fish and other water-living animals to breathe underwater.

hibernation: A resting state, like a deep sleep, that some animals go into during the winter.

mantle: The fold of skin on the body of a snail or slug that protects most of the organs in its body.

mate: When male and female animals come together to produce young.

mollusk: A family of animals with soft, wet bodies, including snails, slugs, clams, mussels, and octopuses.

mucus: The sticky slime produced by a snail or slug as it moves, which protects its body.

muscle: A part of an animal's body that helps it to move.

organ: An important body part, such as the heart, lung, or brain.

pest: An animal or insect that damages plants.

smuggle: To bring something into a country secretly and illegally.

sole: The flat underside of a foot.

spiral: A curved line that starts in the middle and goes around and around getting further away from the center.

spire: A long cone that is pointed at one end.

tentacle: A slender, soft part of an animal's body that is often sensitive to touch.

varnish: See-through, paint-like material that dries to form a shiny coating.

venom: The poison used by some animals to kill the creatures that they hunt.

Further resources

Books

Blaxland, Beth. *Mollusks.* New York: Chelsea House, 2002.
A look at mollusks in general, with information about how snails and slugs sense the world around them, eat, and defend themselves.

Gilpin, Daniel. *Snails, Shellfish, & Other Mollusks.* Minneapolis: Compass Point Books, 2006.
An introduction to all kinds of mollusk, from the common garden snail to the giant squid.

Gray, Susan Heinrichs. *Giant African Snail.* Ann Arbor: Cherry Lake Publishing, 2008.
A look at how giant African snails have destroyed field crops and flower gardens and what is being done to control their spread.

Pyers, Greg. *Snails Up Close.* Chicago: Heinemann Raintree, 2005.
A close look at the lives of snails, with pictures and information about what they are, where they live, and how they feed, reproduce, and avoid enemies.

Web sites

Backyard Nature, "Snails and slugs" *http://www.backyardnature.net/snail_sl.htm*
This is a useful guide to snails and slugs, with close-up photographs of their bodies.

Identification Guide to Land Snails and Slugs of Western Washington,
http://academic.evergreen.edu/projects/ants/TESCBiota/mollusc/key/webkey.htm
This Web site is an excellent introduction to the many kinds of snails and slugs living in North-west America. Similar guides to other states can be found on the Internet.

Snails and Slugs, *http://oregonstate.edu/dept/nurspest/mollusks.htm*
This Web site is devoted to species that have been introduced from other parts of the world, including many common backyard species.

The Apple Snail, *http://fl.biology.usgs.gov/sofla/Apple_Snail/apple_snail.html*
This site is full of information about the Florida apple snail—one of the most interesting of the water snails, and an important part of the Everglades wildlife.

Index